BOW HUNTING

BY ELLEN FRAZEL

BELLWETHER ... LIS, MN

Jump into the cockpit and take flight with Pilot books. Your journey will take you on high-energy adventures as you learn about all that is wild, weird, fascinating, and fun!

This edition first published in 2013 by Bellwether Media, Inc.

No part of this publication may be reproduced in whole or in part without written permission of the publisher. For information regarding permission, write to Bellwether Media, Inc., Attention: Permissions Department, 5357 Penn Avenue South, Minneapolis, MN 55419.

Library of Congress Cataloging-in-Publication Data

Frazel, Ellen.
Bow hunting / by Ellen Frazel.
    pages cm – (Pilot. outdoor adventures)
 Includes bibliographical references and index.
 Summary: "Engaging images accompany information about bow hunting. The combination of high-interest subject matter and narrative text is intended for students in grades 3 through 7"– Provided by publisher.
 ISBN 978-1-60014-889-7 (hardcover : alk. paper)
 1. Bowhunting–Juvenile literature. I. Title.
 SK36.F73 2013
 799.2'15–dc23
                              2012035265

Printed in the United States of America, North Mankato, MN.

TABLE OF CONTENTS

The Bow and Big Game 4

Bow Hunting Equipment 8

Methods and Practice 14

Rules and Respect 18

Hunting the Australian
  Outback 20

Glossary 22

To Learn More 23

Index 24

THE BOW AND BIG GAME

It is a cold day on the Alaska **Peninsula**. On the bank of a creek, a brown bear splashes its big paws in the water. It is fishing for salmon. It does not notice the two bow hunters hiding in the nearby brush. They are waiting for a good shot.

Suddenly the bear rears up on its hind legs. It looks to be about 10 feet (3 meters) tall. The hunters hold their breath as the huge animal steps toward them. One stands up and releases his arrow. It pierces the bear's chest. The wounded animal stumbles away, but the hunters know the shot was **fatal**. They track the bear and find it dead a couple hundred feet away. They have a prize kill!

Trophy Size

Hunters have a scoring system for large trophy animals. The score of a trophy bear is the width plus the length of the bear's skull.

Bow hunting is a method of hunting **game** that involves **archery**. Experienced hunters take up bow hunting for its unique challenges. Some head to **hunting ranches** where professionals lead them on guided hunts. Professionals can also teach beginners the basics of the sport. It takes a lot of practice to master the bow.

The bow has been used since ancient times. Early hunters used bows and arrows to kill animals for food. They made arrows out of pine and other kinds of wood. A hard rock called flint was used to sharpen arrows. Bows and arrows became less popular when firearms became hunting tools in the 1500s. However, those people who loved archery did not leave the bow behind. Over time, they developed more advanced bows and arrows to use for sport.

BOW HUNTING EQUIPMENT

All bows have the same basic parts. Every bow is made with a string attached to a curved bow. An arrow is placed on the string. To shoot the arrow, a hunter pulls the string back and then releases it. Most bows have a peep sight. This is a small plastic circle in the bow string. Hunters look through the peep sight to view their target and line up their shot. Many hunters now use a more advanced **scope**. They also use **range finders** to calculate the distance of their shot.

scope

longbow

Today, most hunters use advanced bows that have a device that helps pull the string. However, some hunters still take on the challenge of traditional bows. **Recurve bows** and **longbows** have no drawing devices. They require hunters to rely on their own strength.

compound bow

Compound bows and crossbows have devices that draw the string. The compound bow is the most popular among bow hunters. It has cables and little wheels called cams that help the hunter pull the string back. This pulley system allows the arrow to be released with extra force.

The crossbow is a small bow mounted to a **stock**. The drawn string is held in place until the hunter lines up a shot. The hunter then presses a trigger to release the arrow. Like the compound bow, the crossbow is fast and **accurate**.

Swift as an Arrow

The best bows give their arrows incredible speed. Some arrows can travel as fast as 355 feet (108 meters) per second.

crossbow

The arrows used in bow hunting are typically made out of **carbon**. This material is very strong and durable. Arrows can also be made of wood or aluminum. Some people make their own arrows. They sharpen stones into points to use as **broadheads**.

All arrows have several basic parts. The nock is the part of the arrow that keeps it in place on the bow string. On the front of the arrow shaft is the insert. This is where a broadhead or a **field point** can be attached. Fletching can be found on the tail end of the arrow. Fletching is made with real or plastic feathers. It makes the arrow rotate in the air. This steers it straight to a target.

broadhead

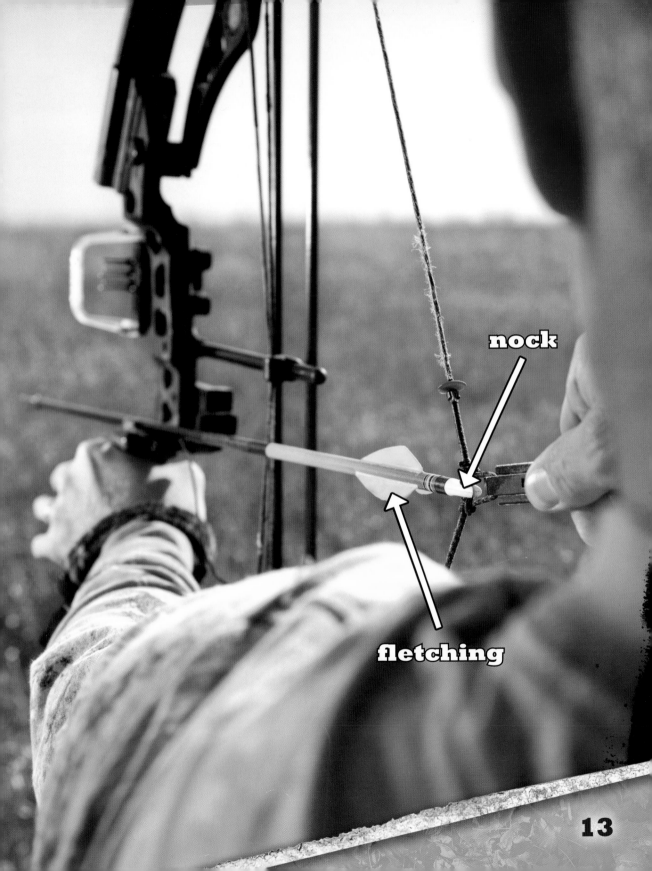

nock

fletching

METHODS AND PRACTICE

Bow hunters use many methods to get animals in position for the perfect shot. Some hunters stalk their game across land. They follow footprints or other signs of movement. Other hunters **bait** animals. Many make animal calls to attract game.

One of the most popular methods used by bow hunters is stand hunting. This is most often used for hunting deer. A hunter waits in a tree stand or elevated **blind** near a source of food or water. When an animal approaches, the hunter waits until it is within 42 yards (38 meters) to take a shot. The **effective kill range** depends on a hunter's choice of bow and skill level.

tree stand

Waiting It Out

Patience is an important part of stand hunting. Hunters must be prepared to wait for hours for a perfect shot.

Experienced bow hunters consider wind and weather conditions. Hunters do not want animals to smell them. They make sure to walk into the wind. That way their scent isn't traveling toward the game.

The best bow hunters also spend time scouting. Skilled deer hunters scout just after deer season ends. They note the spots where deer have scraped trees with their antlers. The hunters return to those spots a few days before the season opens again. They look for fresh marks. Success in bow hunting depends on understanding an animal's habits and routines.

Dressed for the Chill

It is good for bow hunters to practice shooting while wearing heavy clothing. This prepares them for hunting in cold weather.

RULES AND RESPECT

Bow hunters travel to different states for different adventures. Each state sets its own rules and hunting season for each type of game. Hunters go to Alaska and Canada to hunt bears and moose. Deer and turkeys are abundant in Midwestern states. Texas and Florida are popular destinations for hog hunting. In some southern states, people even hunt stingrays and alligators with bows!

Respect for fellow hunters is an important part of bow hunting. Hunters stay out of one another's way. Bow hunters also make sure they do not disturb animal habitats. They try not to leave any items or scents behind. Most importantly, bow hunters do not take shots at animals that are out of their range. It is irresponsible to leave an animal wounded.

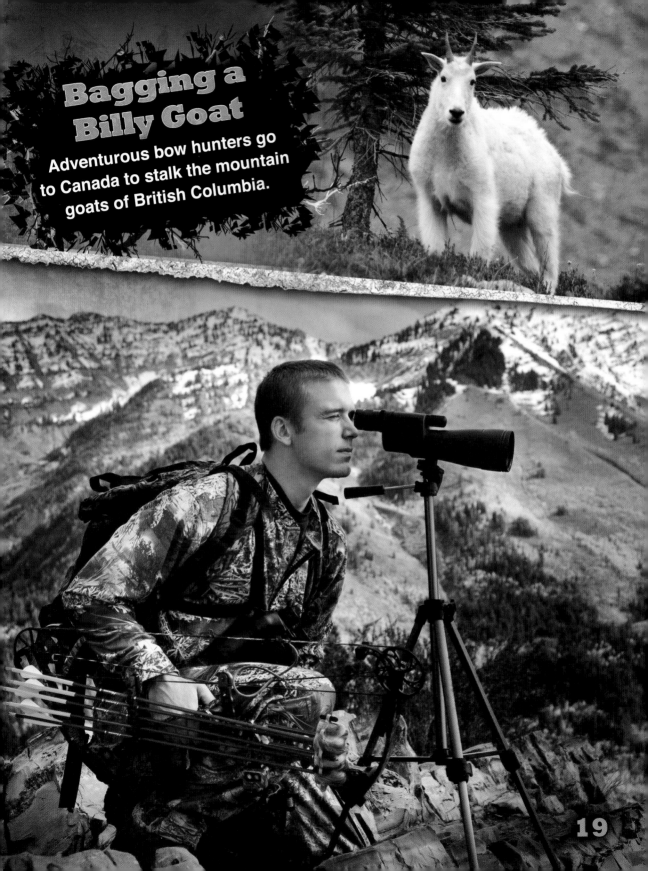

Bagging a Billy Goat

Adventurous bow hunters go to Canada to stalk the mountain goats of British Columbia.

HUNTING THE AUSTRALIAN OUTBACK

The Australian outback is a great place to try the sport of bow hunting. The Australian Bowhunters Association has a coaching program that teaches people the correct way to practice archery. Hunters receive a certificate when they complete the training.

Once certified, hunters can try to capture deer, wild boars, and other Australian game. Experienced hunters who want a big challenge can stalk Asiatic water buffalo. These huge animals weigh between 1,500 and 2,600 pounds (680 and 1,180 kilograms). Their long, curved horns stretch up to 5 feet (1.5 meters) from tip to tip. For a bow hunter, there is nothing quite like shooting an arrow and watching this majestic creature fall!

GLOSSARY

accurate—exact

archery—the art and practice of shooting arrows with a bow

bait—to lure an animal into a hunting area with food or other items

blind—a camouflaged structure that shelters a hunter waiting for game

broadheads—sharp arrowheads used during a hunt

carbon—a hard, durable element used to make arrows and many other common tools

effective kill range—the range of distance from which a bow hunter can successfully kill an animal

fatal—deadly

field point—an arrow tip that is not sharp; field points are practice tips that can be attached to the insert of the arrow shaft.

game—animals hunted for food or sport

hunting ranches—large plots of land where game animals are kept in order to be hunted; hunting ranches usually offer guided hunting tours.

longbows—large traditional bows that have a D-shape

peninsula—a section of land that extends out from a larger piece of land and is almost completely surrounded by water

range finders—hand-held devices that hunters use to calculate the distance between themselves and their target

recurve bows—large traditional bows with tips that curve away from the hunter

scope—a small lens that can be attached to a bow; a hunter uses a scope to sight his or her target.

scouting—exploring a hunting area to learn more about the habits of the animals that live there

stock—the stick on which a crossbow is mounted; the stock contains a device that holds the drawn bow string.

TO LEARN MORE

At the Library

Adamson, Thomas K. *Bowhunting*. Mankato, Minn.: Capstone Press, 2011.

Gunderson, Jessica. *Bowhunting for Fun!* Minneapolis, Minn.: Compass Point Books, 2009.

Howard, Melanie A. *Bowhunting for Kids*. North Mankato, Minn.: Capstone Press, 2012.

On the Web

Learning more about bow hunting is as easy as 1, 2, 3.

1. Go to www.factsurfer.com.

2. Enter "bow hunting" into the search box.

3. Click the "Surf" button and you will see a list of related Web sites.

With factsurfer.com, finding more information is just a click away.

INDEX

archery, 7, 20

arrows, 4, 7, 8, 10, 11, 12, 20

Australian outback, 20

baiting, 14

bears, 4, 5, 18

blind, 14

bows, 7, 8, 9, 10, 11, 12, 14, 18

broadheads, 12

Canada, 18, 19

compound bow, 10, 11

crossbow, 10, 11

deer, 14, 16, 18, 20

effective kill range, 14, 18

field point, 12

fletching, 12, 13

game, 7, 14, 16, 18, 20

hunting methods, 14

hunting ranches, 7

insert, 12

longbow, 9

nock, 12, 13

peep sight, 8

range finder, 8

recurve bow, 9

respect, 18

rules, 18

scent, 16, 18

scope, 8

scoring, 5

scouting, 16

speed, 11

stalking, 14, 19

stand hunting, 14, 15

states, 4, 18

string, 8, 9, 10, 11, 12

tree stand, 14, 15

weather, 16

wind, 16

The images in this book are reproduced through the courtesy of: RubberBall/SuperStock, front cover, pp. 5 (right), 19 (bottom), 21 (right); Nate A., p. 1 (background); Tony Campbell, p. 5 (left); Brad Herndon/Windigo Images, pp. 6-7, 16-17; Mitch Kezar/Windigo Images, pp. 8, 9, 11, 14-15; Marcel Jancovic, p. 10; Keith Publicover, p. 12 (left); shootz photography, p. 12 (right); Fotosearch/Getty Images, p. 13; Sebastien Burel, p. 19 (top); Simon Grosset/Alamy, p. 21 (left).